Client Satisfaction

Guidelines for assessing the quality of leprosy services
from the clients' perspective

Client Satisfaction

Guidelines for assessing the quality of leprosy services from the clients' perspective

Marieke van Dijk

Royal Tropical Institute - Amsterdam
Projects Department Netherlands Leprosy Relief

Netherlands Leprosy Relief (NLR)
Projects Department
P.O. Box 95005
1090 HA Amsterdam
the Netherlands
Telephone: +31 (0)20 5950 500
Telefax: +31 (0)20 6680 823
E-mail: info@leprastichting.nl
Website: www.leprastichting.nl

Royal Tropical Institute (KIT)
KIT Publishers
P.O. Box 95001
1090 HA Amsterdam
the Netherlands
Telephone: +31 (0)20 5688 272
Telefax: +31 (0)20 5688 286
E-mail: publishers@kit.nl
Website: www.kit.nl/publishers

Editor: Leonie McCann
Photography: Marieke van Dijk
Cover and graphic design:
Grafisch Ontwerpbureau Agaatsz BNO,
Meppel, the Netherlands
Printing: Giethoorn Ten Brink, Meppel,
the Netherlands

ISBN: 90 6832 721 6
NUR: 130/890

Contents

'One morning, when I wanted to take my medicine for leprosy, I discovered a rat had been eating the tablets. So I went to another health centre to get a new packet, but they told me I had no leprosy and was not taking the right medicine. With my husband I went to the health centre where I was being treated, but there they got a bit angry with me for not having taken my tablets. They would not give me new medicine. Finally, my husband had to travel all the way to the referral clinic to get new medicine for me.'
Mrs S, Nepal

'I know there are so many cases of leprosy in my village. I have leprosy myself and I recognise their symptoms. I keep telling them to go to the health centre to be checked, but they cannot go. They don't have the money to pay for the transport costs. In my opinion, the health centre should support them with the transport costs.'
Mr P, Nepal

'When I was diagnosed with leprosy, I cried and cried. I thought my body was going to fall apart. They gave me medicine in the health centre. Though my patches started to disappear, I felt very depressed and I stopped going to the health centre to get the medicine. I thought I was going to die anyway. But after some months, I received a letter from the health centre, in which they invited me back for treatment!
I decided to go, because the letter meant that they really cared and had not forgotten about me. The letter was very supportive. Now I'm feeling much better, I was explained the disease is curable and I believe it now!'
Dona G, Brazil

Preface

Every year over half a million new leprosy patients are detected. Since transmission in high endemic countries has not been substantially interrupted, in the coming years considerable numbers of leprosy patients will continue to report to health facilities. Hence, it is crucial that adequate health services are provided to leprosy patients. To ensure that such services remain of good quality, feedback from patients and community, i.e. the 'clients' of the health services, is important. Assessing their experiences and identifying their constraints, as illustrated in the above examples, can help in the further improvement of leprosy services.

Often, however, the clients' perspective of the health services is not systematically assessed. During end evaluations of leprosy control programmes, there is often insufficient time to interview a reasonable number of clients. Large-scale surveys, on the other hand, are usually unfeasible or too expensive. As an initiative of the Netherlands Leprosy Relief (NLR), a workgroup was formed to develop guidelines to study 'client satisfaction' in leprosy services. This booklet 'Guidelines for assessing the quality of leprosy services from the clients' perspective' is the result of this process.

The guidelines were pre-tested between March 2001 and January 2002 in 3 NLR-supported projects (Eastern Region of Nepal, Far Western Region of Nepal and Minas Gerais in Brazil). An attempt was made to set up the study in such a way that it suits most countries' realities. Future use of and experiences with the guidelines will undoubtedly show how and where they can be improved.

Therefore, suggestions and comments on these guidelines are welcome. They should be addressed to:

Netherlands Leprosy Relief (NLR)
Projects Department
P.O. Box 95005
1090 HA Amsterdam
the Netherlands
E-mail: info@leprastichting.nl

The workgroup which facilitated the development of these guidelines consisted of: Marieke van Dijk, Main Researcher of this project, Jan Visschedijk, Public Health Specialist of KIT, Jan Willem Dogger, Project Officer NLR and Anke van der Kwaak, Assistant Professor of the Health Care and Culture Section of the VU Medical Centre. Furthermore, for the development of the methodology some concepts of the study "Gender, leprosy and leprosy control" by KIT/NLR have been used. Though many others contributed to the development of these guidelines, special thanks go to the staff of the 3 collaborating projects, for their valuable assistance.

Marieke van Dijk
Projects Department, NLR

List of abbreviations

FGD	Focus Group Discussion
HF	Health Facility
ILEP	The International Federation of Anti-Leprosy Associations
KIT	Koninklijk Instituut voor de Tropen (Royal Tropical Institute)
MB	Multibacillary
MDT	Multi-Drug Therapy
NLR	Netherlands Leprosy Relief
PB	Paucibacillary
POD	Prevention of Disabilities
RFT	Released From Treatment
VU	Vrije Universiteit (Free University)
WHO	World Health Organisation

Introduction

Leprosy is still a public health problem in many countries. Through leprosy control programmes much effort is being made to ensure a high quality of health services for leprosy patients. To this end, leprosy control programmes are regularly evaluated. Client views and judgements on health services are a vital part of a good understanding of the quality of the programmes. In order to include the clients´ perspective in end evaluations, it is important to conduct studies to assess 'client satisfaction' in leprosy control programmes. These guidelines describe how such a study can be set up and carried out.

Why assess client satisfaction?
End evaluations of leprosy control programmes aim to assess the inputs, process, outcomes and, eventually, the impact of health care interventions. Sometimes the emphasis may lie more on analysing the 'objective' impact of the programme, in terms of gains in health, for instance expressed in epidemiological indicators.

However, the purpose of interventions is not only to increase the health of populations and to enhance equity in health and health care, but also to meet the felt needs and desires of patients and communities. 'Client satisfaction' is increasingly recognised as an important issue in health care quality assessments. Satisfaction with respect to the health services is, besides a goal in itself, also an important precondition for achieving other objectives. Patient awareness and the motivation to consult health facilities are strongly influenced by expectations and satisfaction with the health services. Their perspective is important to understand health seeking behaviour and can help to strengthen early detection and adequate adherence to treatment.

As end evaluations are mostly conducted within a short time-span, they often do not allow for a systematic incorporation of the clients' perspective of the programme. Therefore, a more in-depth study is required prior to an end evaluation, in order to ensure that the most crucial issues of client satisfaction are identified and assessed. The results and recommendations of the study can be used as additional information in end evaluations of leprosy control programmes. However, such a study can also be implemented as a separate activity, independent of the main programme; it is not strictly connected to end evaluations.

The study concerns leprosy patients (the ´primary´ clients), but also involves community members, being 'potential' clients, and health staff members, in order to contrast their point of view with that of the clients.

The objectives of this study are to:

- Assess the quality of the leprosy services from the clients' perspective.
- Identify the clients' priorities among a range of quality aspects of leprosy services.
- Compare the perspective of the clients (patients and community) and the health staff on the quality aspects.
- Formulate recommendations to improve leprosy services.

The expected outputs of the study are:

- Written report.
- Debriefing and discussion of results with the staff of the leprosy control programme.

What quality aspects of the leprosy services does the study cover?

To obtain an idea of the clients' perspective on the quality of the leprosy services, a range of aspects relating to the quality of these services should be covered. In this context, health seeking behaviour is not regarded as a quality aspect in itself, but is directly related to the quality of the health services. It has therefore been included in the study.

The quality aspects under study are:

1. Health seeking behaviour (use of self- or traditional care, patient and doctors' delay)
2. Health education to community (quality, method)
3. Accessibility (costs, waiting time)
4. Condition of facilities (building, cleanliness, toilets)
5. Diagnostic procedures (privacy, dealing with gender difference)
6. Information to patients (quality, method)
7. Contact examination
8. Health staff attitude, continuity and technical competence
9. Treatment (availability of drugs, dealing with non-compliance)
10. Prevention of disabilities (quality, advice/attitude of staff)
11. Stigma and socio-economic consequences (advice on dealing with stigma)

Phases of the study

The study can be divided into three phases: 1) planning and preparation of the study, 2) field work and 3) analysis and report writing. The first phase as outlined in these guidelines will help the manager of the leprosy control programme to set up the study. Under the second and third phases an explanation is given of the steps which the researchers should follow in carrying out the study. The start of the field work phase (day '0') should be planned 3 months before the end evaluation (if applicable).

Phase 1. Planning and preparation

Period	Action	Responsible person(s)
Year before end evaluation	• 1.1 Plan the study period	Programme manager
	• 1.2 Prepare budget and include, when relevant, in the Plan of Activities	
	• 1.3 Request approval from the Ministry of Health, if necessary	
-120 days	• 1.4 Select 2 researchers	Programme manager
-60 days	• 1.5 Plan logistics	Programme manager
-14 days	• 1.6 Translate questionnaires, if necessary	
	• 1.7 Copy questionnaires and prepare 'priority cards'	Programme manager

Phase 2. Field work

Period	Action	Responsible person(s)
Day '0'	• 2.1 Organise preparatory meeting	Programme manager
	• 2.2 Select districts and health facilities within programme area	Research team
	• 2.3 Inform health facilities of the visit dates	
	• 2.4 Discuss methodology and data analysis	
Day 1-6	• 2.5 Select respondents and conduct interviews	Research team
Day 7-8	• 2.6 Conduct focus group discussions	Research team

Phase 3. Analysis and report writing

Period	Action	Responsible person(s)
Day 9-19	• 3.1 Analyse data	Research team
	• 3.2 Write report	
Day 20	• 3.3 Submit report to programme manager	Research team
Day 26	• 3.4 Discuss results with programme staff	Research team
	• 3.5 Submit report to relevant stakeholders	Programme manager

These guidelines will cover each of the phases in turn, and will describe the different steps within each phase.

Important issues to be considered

Before starting the study, some important issues should first be considered. These are briefly discussed below.

Data collection

Traditionally, research on health services is done with the use of quantitative data collection techniques. Quantitative surveys permit the collection of data from large numbers of people. Results are amenable to statistical analysis and can be generalised to wider populations.

For the purpose of assessing client satisfaction, however, a more in-depth and more rapid understanding of opinions, perceptions and motivations is needed. The study, based on a limited study population, should result in a reasonably accurate impression of client satisfaction with regard to the health services offered. Therefore, qualitative data collection techniques are chosen, viz. semi-structured interviews with 20 to 25 leprosy patients and two Focus Group Discussions (FGDs) with 5 to 8 patients. In addition, 6 health staff members and 6 community members are interviewed.

Throughout the whole study, data from interviews and FGDs will be complemented by observation, informal conversations and available information. Observation will give an impression of, for instance, the cleanliness of health facilities, the attitude of health staff members, etc. Informal conversations with health staff members, clients, the programme manager or other key informants can give additional information on the functioning of the leprosy services or perceived problems and constraints. If required, progress reports or other available documentation can be used to gain an impression of the overall leprosy control programme to which the study relates.

Through the combination of these data collection methods (triangulation), the data can be cross-checked and compared for inconsistencies.

'Satisfaction' and 'socially desirable' answers

'Satisfaction' studies involve some important methodological concerns. In general, clients are reluctant to express complaints about their health services and tend to withhold critical comments. They tend to give 'socially desirable' answers, as positive comments are in their own interest for the continuation of care. The identity of the interviewers, as representatives of the leprosy programme, reinforces this effect. This often results in 'highly satisfied' responses, not representing the real situation.

In this study, 'client satisfaction' is conceptualised as 'the quality of the leprosy services from the clients´ perspective'. Rather than asking clients whether they are satisfied or dissatisfied, open-ended questions will be posed on actual experiences and they will be asked their opinions and perceptions on a range of aspects and elements of the leprosy services. They will be invited to suggest improvements, which might disclose the clients 'needs'. Nonetheless, socially desirable answers can never be avoided completely.

The patients' priorities

Patients' ideas regarding priorities in health services often differ from the providers' priorities. For example, it might well be possible that patients prefer a doctor who is less technically competent, but is interested and attentive, rather than a technically skilled, but rude physician. Low quality of such aspects might be a reason for avoiding leprosy services and defaulting. Information on patient priorities can give an indication as to where quality improvement might be most gainful.

Therefore, a simple system of defining priorities has been incorporated in the study. Quality aspects relating to the leprosy services have been printed on cards. At the end of the interview, the patient will be asked to choose 3 cards that display the most important quality aspects regarding the leprosy services, according to his/her opinion. Discussion of the chosen cards can give valuable information on the patients' concerns. Furthermore, patients will be given the opportunity to express additional issues of importance for them, which have not been discussed during the interview.

Representativeness

A compromise has to be found between the extent of the study and its feasibility in terms of time, money and manpower. The study strives to obtain reasonably valid and reliable information that gives insight into the quality of the services from the clients' point of view. However, it does not claim to be fully representative. The study will be conducted on a small-scale and within a short time-span. The amount of persons interviewed is relatively small, sampling may not be completely at random, and informal interviewing approaches are used. Striking results could be further investigated and quantified. Any possible bias should be taken into account in the analysis and mentioned in the report.

Ethical considerations

Some principles need to be adhered to, in order to prevent that any harm is done. The anonymity and confidentiality of the respondent should be ensured. Before the interview begins, the researcher should provide adequate information on the objectives of the research, and should ask the respondent for his/her permission to be included in the study. Numbers are given to respondents. Privacy should be ensured during the interviews as much as possible. Sensitive issues should only be explored when a good relation has been established with the respondent during the interview.

Phase 1: Planning and preparation

The programme manager co-ordinates the first phase of the study. (S)he should start preparations one year before the end evaluation (if applicable).

Steps for planning and preparation
1.1 Plan the study period
1.2 Prepare budget and include, when relevant, in the Plan of Activities
1.3 Request approval from the Ministry of Health, if necessary
1.4 Select 2 researchers
1.5 Plan logistics
1.6 Translate questionnaires, if necessary
1.7 Copy questionnaires and prepare 'priority cards'

Step 1.1 Plan the study period (year before end evaluation)
In the year before the end evaluation of the programme will take place, the programme manager should plan the period in which the study will be conducted. The study takes about 4 weeks in total, depending on the size of the study area and the experience of the researchers. The study should commence at least 3 months before the end evaluation starts, as the report on the results of the study should be available 2 months before the end evaluation.

Step 1.2 Prepare budget and include, when relevant, in the Plan of Activities (year before end evaluation)
The programme manager prepares a tentative budget for the study and includes this, when relevant, in the Plan of Activities for the year in which the study will take place. Budget items that may have to be included are:
- Allowances/per diems researchers
- Travel of researchers to the study area
- Transport costs during the study
- Hotel costs for 2 researchers
- Photocopying and printing costs
- Materials (tape recorder, pens, paper, markers)
- Translation costs (questionnaires/guidelines/report)
- Refreshments for participants FGDs/respondents
- Refunding of travel expenses for participants FGDs

Step 1.3 Request approval from the Ministry of Health, if necessary (year before end evaluation)
In some countries, approval for carrying out this study may be needed from the co-ordinator of the national leprosy control programme at the Ministry of Health. If this is the case, the programme manager should send a letter to the person(s) concerned, in which the purpose of the study is explained and permission for conducting the study is requested.

In some countries, permission from an 'ethical committee for research' may also be required. The programme manager should investigate, timely in advance, whether this applies to his/her country, and should follow the necessary procedures.

Step 1.4 Select 2 researchers (-120 days)
The programme manager identifies the research team. To have sufficient time to find suitable and available researchers, (s)he should start selecting researchers about 4 months before the start of the study. The programme manager stays in regular contact with the team and oversees the proceedings of the study, from the planning and preparation stage to the production of the final report.

Two researchers are needed to conduct the study: the first researcher should be a senior leprosy supervisor, programme manager, or other leprosy control expert. However, (s)he should preferably not be involved in the leprosy control programme under study The second researcher should be a social scientist. Both researchers should be independent from the health facilities that will be visited in order to prevent socially desirable answers and biased report writing. It is crucial that both researchers have good interviewing skills, are capable of analysing data, and are objective. The success of the study depends highly on the researchers!

The first researcher (1) should
- Be a senior leprosy supervisor, programme manager, or other leprosy control expert, but not involved in the leprosy control programme under study
- Have good knowledge of leprosy and leprosy control
- Have experience with community work
- Have good communication and interviewing skills
- Have knowledge of the local language(s) and English
- Preferably have knowledge on doing research

The second researcher (2) should
- Be a social scientist or have significant experience with social sciences (or health systems research)
- Have experience with interviews, focus group discussions and data analysis
- Have experience with community work
- Have good communication and interviewing skills
- Have knowledge of the local language(s) and English
- Preferably have knowledge of leprosy and leprosy care

Researcher 1 can be recruited from governmental or non-governmental organisations working with leprosy control in the country. To find researcher 2, research institutes, faculties of social sciences, etc., can be contacted.

Once 2 researchers have been found who are capable, willing and available to do this study, they should be given these guidelines to read in advance. If the researchers are unfamiliar with the leprosy control programme under study, the programme manager will inform them of its objectives and activities. When necessary, the social scientist should be provided with additional information on leprosy, for example in the form of basic health education materials. The learning guide published by ILEP called: 'How to Diagnose and Treat Leprosy' (2001) is also useful for this purpose.

Tasks and responsibilities

Researcher 1 will bring the necessary expertise on leprosy and knowledge of leprosy programmes in general and will inform researcher 2 about the most crucial aspects of leprosy and leprosy control. Methodological input will be given by researcher 2, who exchanges his/her knowledge on qualitative research methods and data analysis with researcher 1.

Both researchers will help the programme manager to organise the study. The first 3 interviews and both FGDs will be done by the two researchers together. The remaining interviews will be done by each researcher individually.

It is advisable to determine in advance which of the two researchers will be responsible for writing the report. However, the conclusions and recommendations of the report should be jointly discussed and the final report should have both researchers' agreement.

Step 1.5 Plan logistics (-60 days)

Transport, accommodation and other arrangements should be organised by the programme manager before the start of the study:

- Allowances/per diems researchers
- Transport of researchers to study area
- Transport of researcher within study area
- Hotel reservations for researchers
- Administrative support (computer, printer, photocopy facilities)
- Equipment and supplies (paper, pens, 'priority cards', markers, tape recorder, diskettes)
- Office accommodation for researchers

Step 1.6 Translate questionnaires, if necessary (-14 days)

In most countries the questionnaires will need to be translated into the local language. The programme manager is responsible for arranging the translation. The person translating the questions should have adequate knowledge of leprosy and research methodology. Instead of a literal translation, the questions should be translated in such a way that the meaning of the question remains the same as in the original version. Sufficient space should be left in which answers can be noted. After translating the questionnaires, the translation and interpretation of the questions should be checked and corrected where necessary by a different person (e.g. one of the researchers).

Step 1.7 Copy questionnaires and prepare 'priority cards' (-14 days)
The programme manager ensures that sufficient copies of the translated questionnaires (25 for patients, 6 for community members and 6 for health staff) are made, and that 8 complete sets of priority cards are prepared (see annex 5).

Phase 2: Field work

The programme manager is responsible for organising a preparatory meeting. The remaining steps will mainly be carried out by the researchers.

Steps for field work
2.1 Organise preparatory meeting
2.2 Select districts and health facilities within programme area
2.3 Inform health facilities of the visit dates
2.4 Discuss methodology and data analysis
2.5 Conduct interviews
2.6 Conduct focus group discussions

Step 2.1 Organise preparatory meeting (day 0)
A preparatory meeting should be organised by the programme manager. (S)he should invite the 2 researchers and other stakeholders who will be involved. All should be provided with a copy of these guidelines to read in advance. The programme manager gives a short briefing to the participants of the meeting, including the following issues:

Agenda of the preparatory meeting:
1. Welcome, introduction participants
2. Explanation of the purpose and methodology of the study by the programme manager
3. Discussion of questions or remarks on the procedures of the study
4. Definition of responsibilities of both researchers according to 1.4
5. Selection of districts to be visited according to 2.2
6. Selection of 6 health facilities in the chosen districts, to carry out the interviews according to 2.2
7. Selection of health facilities to conduct the FGDs according to 2.8
8. Formulation of tentative agenda for visits to the health facilities
9. Provision of additional background information needed for the study to the researchers by the programme manager (e.g. annual report, information on leprosy)

In principle, this meeting takes place on the day preceding the start of the interviews. However, if it is more appropriate to select and inform the health facilities longer in advance, then the programme manager should try to plan the preparatory meeting for an earlier date. If this is not possible, e.g. due to the fact that the researchers live too far away to travel for this meeting only, then the programme manager should make a tentative selection of health facilities, inform these facilities in advance about the study and agree upon a day for the visit (see 2.3). In this case, the preparatory meeting can be held as planned on the day before the start of interviews, and the tentative schedule can then be confirmed or adapted.

Step 2.2 Select districts and health facilities within programme area (day 0)
The study aims to cover a representative sample of districts (or local government areas/municipalities/etc.) in the programme area. If programmes cover very large areas, it will only be possible to look at a few selected parts. In that case, preference is given to 3 or 4 districts of the programme area that have the highest amount of leprosy patients.

All types of health facilities offering leprosy services that fall under the responsibility of the programme, are included in the sample: health centres, health posts, sub-health centres, referral hospitals and other leprosy treatment centres. In the chosen districts, a selection of in total 6 health facilities will be made in such a way that this includes

- Large and small health facilities
- Facilities in urban and rural settings
- Facilities with easy and difficult access
- Facilities with smooth and more problematic functioning

The researchers should strive to obtain a selection of health facilities that can represent the local situation as accurately as possible. The health facilities where the FGDs will be conducted can be either the same or different from those where the interviews are held. The selection of health facilities is made together with the programme manager during the preparatory meeting (see 2.1).

The respondents are the persons who will provide the information needed: leprosy patients, community members and health staff members. In each of the 6 health facilities, it is necessary to interview:

- 3 to 4 leprosy patients (of which one defaulting/irregular patient)
- 1 health staff member
- 1 community member

The selection of respondents is usually made at the time of the visit to the health facility, preceding the interviews. Selection criteria are given in step 2.5.

Step 2.3 Inform health facilities of the visit dates (day 0)
Either the programme manager or the research team contacts the managing health staff member of the selected health facilities and informs him/her of the purposes of the study. They should be invited to participate and a visit should be scheduled, if possible according to the agenda set during the preparatory meeting.

The health staff should be asked to invite a defaulting or irregular patient and a community member on the day of the visit. It should be agreed which health staff member will be interviewed to ensure the person will be present and will have time during the visit of the research team. If less than 3 leprosy patients are expected on the day of the visit, the health staff should be asked to invite patients from the most recent register, according to the criteria mentioned in step 2.5.

Step 2.4 Discuss methodology and data analysis (day 0)
Before starting the interviews, the researchers should discuss the methodology of the study. They prepare the discussion by reading annex 3 to 9 of these guidelines in advance. The social scientist, as the expert on qualitative research, brings in his/her knowledge on interview skills, possible bias, methodology for FGDs and data analysis. The researchers review the checklist for analysis and discuss the plan for data analysis. The leprosy control expert informs the social scientist on leprosy and the main issues of leprosy care.

Step 2.5 Select respondents and conduct interviews (day 1-6)
The study aims to obtain information on the opinions, attitudes and suggestions of respondents. Therefore, interactive interviews using open-ended questions are used for the data collection. Background information on interview skills, explanation of the priority card system, and the questionnaires are attached in annexes 3, 4 and 5. The researchers should read these before they commence the interviews. It is also advisable to read the checklist for analysis (annex 9) before starting the interviews, as this will give an idea of the information eventually needed.

Each interview takes about 45 minutes to one hour. The questionnaires for each of the 3 study populations (patients, community members, health staff members) should be numbered separately. The researchers can do the first 3 interviews (one patient, one health staff member and one community member) together, whereby one is interviewing and the other taking notes. They alternate these roles at every interview. When both interviewers feel that they can handle the interviews alone, they proceed individually, taking notes themselves. They should be able to conduct an average of 3 to 4 interviews per person per day.

Selection leprosy patients
The research team tries to interview 20 to 25 leprosy patients in total. This means that in each of the 6 selected health facilities, 3 to 4 leprosy patients should be interviewed. Preferably all categories of patients should be represented, so as to obtain maximum variation in the sample. This includes:
- Male and female patients
- Patients from different ethnic groups (if applicable)
- PB and MB patients
- Patients in different stages of treatment
- Patients recently released from treatment
- Patients with reactions
- Patients with disabilities
- Defaulting or irregular patients
- Patients who defaulted but have returned to treatment

If there are specific clinic days or consultation times on which leprosy patients are treated, then it is most likely that sufficient leprosy patients can be found to co-operate with the interviews among the waiting patients. If, however, there are no specific clinic days for leprosy patients, the health staff should be asked to invite the patients in advance to attend the clinic on the day of the visit (see 2.3).

Sometimes defaulting/irregular patients may be difficult to find for the interviews. However, given the subject under study, this group in particular can provide valuable information. Their reasons for defaulting may stem from their dissatisfaction with certain aspects of the leprosy services. Therefore, the research team should try to find these patients right from the beginning. They should strive to interview at least one defaulting or irregular patient in each health facility visited.

Selection health staff members

The researchers interview 6 health staff members who treat leprosy patients, i.e. one in each health facility visited. They can be:

- Health workers/paramedicals
- Dermatologists
- Nurses
- Physicians
- Physiotherapists
- Occupational therapists

Selection community members

In the communities where the visited health facilities are situated, one leader or representative of the community should be interviewed In this way, a total of 6 community members will be interviewed during the study. The community member should be able to express the expectations and opinions of his/her community. Possible community members for selection are:

- Village leaders
- Religious leaders
- Schoolteachers
- Members of women's groups

Step 2.6 Conduct focus group discussions (day 7-8)

After finishing all the interviews, 2 FGDs will be organised, each comprising 5 to 8 leprosy patients. Topics are chosen according to interesting issues that arose during the interviews. These themes for discussion can usefully complement the results of the interviews. During the preparatory meeting, it is decided in which 2 health facilities the FGDs will be organised (these may be either 2 of the health facilities where interviews were conducted, or other health facilities). The health facilities should be informed and asked to co-operate in the recruitment of participants. The participants can be selected according to the same criteria as the patients for the interviews. However, the patients participating in the FGDs will preferably be different from those who have been interviewed.

Both researchers should be present at the FGDs: one in the role of facilitator, one in the role of recorder. A FGD typically lasts up to an hour and a half. Directly after the FGD, the main results of the discussion should be summarised. Detailed guidelines for holding FGDs are attached in annex 6; these should be read carefully before organising the FGDs.

A possible agenda could be as follows (HF=health facility):

Day	**Visit**	**Action researcher 1**	**Action researcher 2**
Day 1	HF 1	Interview 1 patient, 1 community member, 1 health staff member (both researchers do interviews together)	
		Interview 1 patient	Interview 1 patient
Day 2	HF 2	Interview 2 patients and 1 health staff member	Interview 2 patients and 1 community member
Day 3	HF 3	Interview 2 patients and 1 community member	Interview 2 patients and 1 health staff member
Day 4	HF 4	Interview 2 patients and 1 health staff member	Interview 2 patients and 1 community member
Day 5	HF 5	Interview 2 patients and 1 community member	Interview 2 patients and 1 health staff member
Day 6	HF 6	Interview 2 patients and 1 health staff member	Interview 2 patients and 1 community member
Day 7	HF X	FGD	
Day 8	HF Y	FGD	

Phase 3: Analysis and report writing

The last part of the study involves data analysis and the writing of the report. The researchers are responsible for conducting this phase of the study.

Steps for analysis and report writing
3.1 Analyse data
3.2 Write report
3.3 Submit report to programme manager
3.4 Discuss results with programme staff
3.5 Submit report to relevant stakeholders

Step 3.1 Analyse data (day 9-19)
Data analysis is the most important, but also the most time-consuming part of the study. In annex 7, an explanation of the analysis of data is given. The researchers should read this carefully before analysing the data. The interviews with the different study populations must be analysed separately, using the attached checklist for analysis (annex 9). The checklist will help to describe and interpret the data and draw conclusions. Researchers who are familiar with the use of master sheets (see example annex 8) can use these to make the data more manageable.

Step 3.2 Write report (day 9-19)
Data analysis goes hand in hand with the writing of the report. Often it can be useful to assign one of the researchers responsibility for writing the report. However, the conclusions and recommendations should be jointly discussed, and the contents of the final report approved by both persons. The report should give a clear and concise overview of the results of this study. Annex 10 shows the recommended format for the report. Some parts of the report (introduction, methodology followed) can already be written during the field work phase. The report should contain the following chapters:

Executive summary
Give a short description of the methodology used. State clearly the main findings and conclusions and the 5-7 most significant recommendations of the study.

Introduction
Give a short introduction describing the aim of the study. Mention the period in which it has been conducted and by whom.

Methodology
Give an overview of the districts and health facilities visited and a short description of the sampling procedures followed. Report the number of interviews and FGDs conducted in each of the health facilities. Outline the background information of the respondents interviewed (number of male and female patients, PB and MB patients, number of patients with disabilities, number of defaulting and irregular patients, occupation of community members and health staff, etc.).

Discuss the representativeness of the study. Practical or methodological problems that could have affected the findings should be reported. Mention the amount of respondents who, for whatever reason, did not participate in the study. Include a short evaluation of your own experiences with and your views on the study (e.g. were these guidelines sufficiently clear? were the data-collection tools adequate? was the time available sufficient? how was the co-operation between the researchers?).

Results
Give a clear presentation of the results. Analyse each quality aspect separately. Always include the amount of respondents who were of the same opinion or gave a similar suggestion, as it is important to know if a suggestion is mentioned by one individual or by a more extended group of respondents. Include interesting remarks and details mentioned by respondents to illustrate the data. After discussing each quality aspect, include a conclusion of the major findings of that aspect in 2 or 3 sentences. List the suggestions for improvement given by the respondents, and add which type of respondent gave the suggestion (patients, participants of FGDs, health staff or community members). Even if you doubt the feasibility of suggestions, it is advisable to include them because they can give a clear idea of the clients' needs, which possibly could be solved in another manner.

Conclusion and recommendations
Draw conclusions from your results, and relate them to the actual functioning of the leprosy programme. Discuss the clients' perspective on the leprosy services and their (dis)satisfaction relating to the several quality aspects. List the most important 5-7 recommendations resulting from the study. These should be clear and concrete.

Annexes
List references used, include a schedule of activities and a map depicting the health facilities visited. Include the results of the priority card system and the topic list used for the FGDs. The questionnaires may also be attached, but if no changes have been made in the questions, then reference can simply be made to the guidelines. In the final report, a summary of the discussion with programme staff should also be included as an annex (step 3.4).

Step 3.3 Submit report to programme manager (day 20)
Once the draft report has been finalised, it should be presented to the programme manager.

Step 3.4 Discuss results with programme staff (day 26)
The researchers discuss the results and recommendations with the programme manager and staff (do they think the results represent the clients' perspective in their programme area? are the recommendations feasible? do significant differences exist in the 'satisfaction' with the various health facilities visited?). A short summary of the outcome of the discussion should be made and attached to the final report as an annex.

Step 3.5 Submit report to relevant stakeholders (day 26)
The programme manager sends the report to all relevant stakeholders, including the evaluation team. They should receive the report about 2 months before the end evaluation of the programme.

Annex 1. Definition of terms and concepts

Bias:	A distortion in the collected data so that it does not represent reality.
Clients of leprosy services:	Leprosy patients and community members.
Client satisfaction:	The quality of health services from the perspective of clients.
Data collection techniques:	Semi-structured interviews with patients, community members and health staff, as well as FGDs with patients.
Data collection tools:	The questionnaires for the interviews and the topics used for the FGDs.
Defaulter:	A patient who can no longer complete MDT regimen, regardless of whether (s)he is still coming to the treatment centre. An MB patient becomes a defaulter as soon as (s)he has missed 13 months of the two-year treatment, or if (s)he has missed 7 months of the one-year treatment. A PB-patient becomes a defaulter as soon as (s)he has missed 4 months of treatment.
District:	An administrative entity in a country. 'District' also implies local equivalents, such as: municipalities, local government areas, etc.
Leprosy services:	Activities of the health services related to the care and cure of leprosy patients.
Focus Group Discussion:	A group discussion guided by a facilitator, during which group members talk freely and spontaneously about a certain topic.

Health facility:	The health unit under study. This can be a sub-health centre, health centre, health post, district hospital, primary health care centre, referral hospital, etc.
Irregular patient:	A leprosy patient who does not come for treatment at the appointed date.
Reliability:	'Repeatability' of the findings: someone else using the same method in the same circumstances should be able to obtain the same findings.
Respondent:	Person that gives information required for the study.
Sampling:	The process of selecting a number of study units from a defined study population.
Semi-structured interview:	Data collection technique that involves oral questioning of respondents. Though there is a standard list of open-ended questions (here called 'questionnaire'), some degree of flexibility is allowed.
Triangulation:	The combination of different data-collection techniques which enables the consideration of problems from different perspectives.
Validity:	When the scientific observations actually measure what they intend to measure.

Annex 2. Key references

1 Bernhart M.H. et al: Patient Satisfaction in developing countries. *Social Science & Medicine*, 1999; 48: 989-996.

2 Campen C. van et al: Quality of Care and Patient Satisfaction: A Review of Measuring Instruments. *Medical Care Research and Review*, 1995; 52(1): 109-133.

3 Campen, C. van et al: Assessing Noninstitutionalized Asthma and COPD Patients' Priorities and Perceptions of Quality of Health Care: The Development of the QUOTE-CNSLD Instrument. *Journal of Asthma*, 1997; 34(6): 531-538

4 Dijk M. van: *Report of the Pilot Study 'Quality of Leprosy Services from the Clients' Perspective' ELCP – Nepal (18 April-12 May 2001)*. June 2001; Amsterdam: Project Department NLR.

5 Dijk M. van: *Report of the Pilot Study 'Quality of Leprosy Services from the Clients' Perspective' Minas Gerais – Brazil (18 June-14 July 2001)*. August 2001; Amsterdam: Project Department NLR.

6 Gilson L. et al: Community satisfaction with primary health care services: an evaluation undertaken in the Morogoro Region of Tanzania. *Social Science & Medicine*, 1994; 39(6): 767-780.

7 Hall J.A., M.C. Dornan: Meta-analysis of satisfaction with medical care: description of research domain and analysis of overall satisfaction levels. *Social Science & Medicine*, 1988; 27(6): 637-644.

8 Hall J.A., M.C. Dornan: Patient sociodemographic characteristics as predictors of satisfaction with medical care: a meta-analysis. *Social Science & Medicine*, 1990; 30(7): 811-818.

9 Hardon A. et al: *Applied Health Research Manual. Anthropology of Health and Health Care*. 1994; Amsterdam: Mahidol University, De La Salle University, Royal Tropical Institute, University of Amsterdam.

10 Linder-Pelz S.: Toward a theory of patient satisfaction. *Social Science and Medicine*, 1982; 16: 577-582.

11 Mendoza Aldana J. et al: Client satisfaction and quality of health care in rural Bangladesh. *Bulletin of World Health Organization*, 2001; 79 (6): 512-517.

12 Pant H.R., S. Dhakal: *'Client Satisfaction' A study to quality aspects related with leprosy services in the Far Western Region*. December 2001; Dhangadhi.

13 Ross C.K. et al: A comparative Study of Seven Measures of Patient Satisfaction. *Medical Care*, 1995; 33(4): 392-406.

14 Sitzia J., N. Wood: Patient satisfaction: a review of issues and concepts. *Social Science & Medicine*, 1997; 45(12): 1829-1843.

15 Sixma H.J. et al: Quality of care from the patients' perspective: from theoretical concept to a new measuring instrument. *Health Expectations*, 1998; I: 82-95.
16 Varkevisser C.M.: *Mission in support of qualitative research for the National Tuberculosis Programme, Eqypt.* 7-12 November 2000; Amsterdam: Royal Tropical Institute.
17 Varkevisser C.M., I. Pathmanathan, A. Brownlee: *Designing and Conducting Health Systems Research Projects.* Draft December 2000; WHO/IDRC.
18 Visschedijk J.: *Proposal for a study to develop a model for assessing 'customer's satisfaction'* . 2000; Amsterdam: Royal Tropical Institute.
19 Williams, B.: Patient satisfaction: a valid concept? *Social Science & Medicine*, 1994; 38(4): 509-516.

Annex 3. Semi-structured interviews[1]

A semi-structured interview is a face-to-face interview using a standard list of open questions (here called 'questionnaire') in which some degree of flexibility during the interview is allowed. For the exploration of opinions and perceptions, the method has important advantages:

Advantages

- Respondents can give free responses, expressed in their own words
- Respondents are given the opportunity to mention issues not previously thought of when the study was designed. This may provide valuable new insights on the issue
- Respondents can be asked to clarify answers, in order to avoid misinterpretation of the information
- Questions can be clarified by the interviewer when necessary
- The method is accessible for both literate and illiterate informants

However, be aware of possible bias when doing the interviews:

Possible bias

- The interviewer has an effect on the respondents' answers. Respondents tend to give answers they think the interviewer likes to hear (socially desirable answers)
- The respondents' answers will be affected by the presence of other persons during the interview
- When asked about events that happened in the past ('when (s)he went to the health facility for the first time', or 'what (s)he knew about leprosy before diagnosis'), respondents may not remember everything exactly (recall bias)
- The interviewer only sees or hears things in which (s)he is interested and misses information that is critical to the study (observer bias)

These potential biases threaten the validity and reliability of the study. By being aware of them it is possible, to a certain extent, to prevent them. If the researchers do not fully succeed, it is important to report honestly in what ways the data may be biased.

[1] The information contained in this annex is based on the Health Systems Research modules developed by Varkevisser et al. For more detailed information, the original modules can be consulted (see key references).

Interview skills
The respondents are possible partners who, with their information, can help to understand better why people behave as they do. To turn a respondent into a partner, the researcher has to invest in the relationship. The following interview skills can help make the interview both acceptable for the respondent and informative for the researcher:

Environment
Try to find a private environment for the interview in the health facility. Any potentially disturbing factors (noise, other people listening, a formal surrounding) should be avoided where possible. Health staff members should be informed in advance that for the sake of the confidentiality, they should not be present during the interviews. If possible, arrange interviews with defaulting patients in a more neutral setting.

Gender sensitivity
Gender relations have to be respected. If the research couple consists of a male and a female researcher, it is preferable that the female researcher interviews female respondents and the male researcher the male respondents.

Attitude of the interviewer
- Be friendly, relaxed, never in a hurry and make the respondent feel at ease
- Listen well, show interest in what the respondent says, maintain eye-contact
- Use simple, everyday language
- Never show any disapproval or surprise over the information received during the interview; otherwise the respondent will close up. The interviewer should only listen and try to understand what people think and why they do what they do. The interviewer can address problems or incorrect information identified during the interviews after the interview is finished.
- Show by verbal and body language that the information received is highly appreciated. Nodding, humming and repeating the last few words may all be perceived as encouragement. A silence from the side of the interviewer may also work as encouragement for the informant to continue.

Note that when something goes 'wrong' in an interview the interviewer should always take the blame. (S)he is the one who 'did not ask the question clearly enough', or who 'did not understand the answer'.

Introduction of the interview
When starting the interview, give a clear introduction about the purpose of the interview and the study, tell the respondent his/her name will not be mentioned and the information will be handled confidentially. Explain why responses have to be written down and mention the expected duration of the interview. Ask the respondents' consent.

If the researchers find this suitable, respondents can be offered some small incentive, for example a cup of tea/coffee.

Posing questions and evaluating answers

The questionnaires for the interviews are included in these guidelines. Remember that the questionnaires are 'tools' or 'instruments' to get certain information. In other words, the interviewers' task is not only to pose questions, but also to evaluate answers and 'probe' for elaboration or more precision in case of a superficial or invalid answer.

It is useful to look through the checklist for analysis (annex 9) before starting the interviews. This will give an idea of the information that should result from the interviews, and which is eventually needed in the final report.

Take care that, when posing questions, you:

- Ask questions in a neutral manner, avoid leading the respondent to believe that one answer would be preferred over another ('leading questions')
- Avoid putting words into the respondent's mouth. The respondent should give the answers him/herself
- Do not present possible answers

Note that, with open-ended questions, more than one answer is allowed. Interviewers have to wait for additional answers. Strive to complete answers and probe when they are unclear or doubtful. An answer can be unsatisfactory in many ways:

- The respondent gives <u>no answer at all</u> because (s)he did not understand the question. Repeat or rephrase the question in such a way that the respondent understands, without providing possible options for responses. Sometimes respondents do not answer because the question touches on sensitive information, which the respondent hesitates to give. In that case, repeat that if (s)he wishes (s)he can skip the question. If the respondent has no objection to continuing, stress that the information will remain confidential.

- The answer may be <u>incomplete</u>, or <u>unclear</u>. In that case, repeat what is said and encourage the respondent to continue or explain further. You can probe with questions such as: 'When was that?', 'Why did you do that?', 'Why do you think so?', etc.

- The answer may be <u>irrelevant</u> to your question. Say something such as 'That is not exactly what I meant to ask about' and repeat the question, slightly elaborated.

- You suspect the respondent is <u>not telling the truth</u> (invalid answer), either because various parts of the answer contradict each other or because the respondent knows the 'desirable' answer and gives it to please the interviewer. If you suspect this is happening, avoid the slightest sign of disbelief or irritation. Summarise the contradictory statements and make clear in a friendly, interested way that you would highly appreciate if the respondent elaborates further.

Noting down answers

Use the space left open in the questionnaires to write down the answers given. The answers do not need to be in English. They can be written down in the local language. It is important not to let your note-taking distract you or the respondent. Try not to summarise, but write answers as completely as possible in the words of the respondent, without sifting or interpreting them. Information provided in the respondent's own words might be useful later as examples or illustrations, which will add interest to the final report.

Leading the discussion

The interviewer has to lead the discussion, but at the same time encourage the respondent to give spontaneous information relevant to the topic by letting him/her talk. If respondents give interesting spontaneous remarks, don't hesitate to step away from the questionnaire and explore these issues; they sometimes provide the most interesting information for the study. However, some spontaneous information may distract from the main issues. In the limited time available (maximum 1 hour), all topics should have been adequately covered, so that the information by different respondents will be comparable. Therefore, an interviewer will sometimes have to stop informants who go enthusiastically off track. This can be done politely: 'Thank you, this is interesting, but do you mind if I go back to the previous (or next) question? This (specify) is not yet fully clear to me.'

Choosing priorities

At the end of each patient interview, put the cards with the quality aspects printed on them on a table in a random order. Explain for each card which issue it represents. State the quality aspects in a positive way, for instance '*short* waiting time', '*adequate* information to patients on their disease'. Ask the patient to choose the three most important quality aspects of leprosy services displayed on the table. Explain that (s)he should choose priorities according to his/her personal opinion. Add that, if the patient wants, you can repeat the aspects printed on each card.

Directly after finishing the interview, tick the quality aspects chosen in the table included in the questionnaire.

Example

Quality aspect	Priority?
Low costs to go to the leprosy services	✔
Short waiting time	
Adequate privacy	
Adequate information to leprosy patients on their disease	✔
Friendly health workers with sufficient time to help	✔
Adequate attention to prevention of disabilities	
Advice by leprosy workers on dealing with the social consequences of leprosy	

Finishing the interview

When the interview has finished, you can respond to any questions that arose during the interviews, give advice (if necessary or requested) and provide the opportunity for further questions from the respondent. If the respondent has no further remarks or questions, thank him/her for participating in the interview. Put away the completed questionnaires before the next interview starts (as they contain confidential information).

Summary

- Find a private environment for the interview
- Give a clear introduction on the interview
- Ask the respondents' consent
- Be friendly and at ease
- Encourage and make the respondent feel at ease
- Use simple, everyday language
- Avoid leading questions
- Maintain eye-contact
- Avoid presenting possible answers
- Listen well, show interest in what the respondent says
- Never show any disapproval or surprise on the information received
- Wait for additional answers
- Strive to complete answers
- Probe when the responses are unclear or doubtful
- Write down complete answers in the respondent´s own words
- Take care the discussion does not take too long
- Patient interviews: ask patient to choose priorities
- Answer questions, thank the respondent

Annex 4. Questionnaires

The next pages contain the questionnaires of the patient interview, the community member interview and the health staff interview. If needed, translate them into the local language. Use the same layout, leaving sufficient space for noting down answers. Make as many photocopies of these translated versions as required.

Patient questionnaire **Pt form nr** ☐

Date of interview: ____________________

Name of interviewer: ____________________

Place and name of health facility: ____________________

'We are interviewing leprosy patients on their experiences with the different health centres in the area. We would like to ask you some questions about your views on the quality of the health services offered here. Your views are very important for us to know because there may be aspects of the services for leprosy patients that can still be improved. The interview will take about 45 minutes to one hour. The information you give us will be handled confidentially and your name will not be mentioned. Would you like to co-operate with this study?
If yes: 'do you mind if we take notes?'

1. Sex (M/F): ____________________

2. Age (in years): ____________________

3. For how long do/did you have to take treatment? ____________________

4. How many doses have you taken until now? ____________________

5. Do you have any impairments or disabilities due to leprosy? What kind of disabilities?

____

____

Health seeking behaviour

6. Before you decided to go to a doctor or health facility, did you try anything at home to get rid of the symptoms? (probe: self-treatment, e.g. with herbs, drugs or ointments from pharmacy, traditional care)

____

____

____

____

7. How much time existed between the start of the disease and the first time you went to a doctor/health facility (for this disease)? (probe: why did you wait? Why did you finally decide to go?)

____

____

____

____

Pt form nr [ ]

8. Where did you go for treatment? (note all visits to private physicians, hospitals, health centres, specifying other diagnosed diseases and where leprosy was diagnosed)

1st visit to: ________________ diagnosis: ________________

If applicable:
2nd visit to: ________________ diagnosis: ________________
3rd visit to: ________________ diagnosis: ________________

9. How much time existed between the first time you went to a doctor/health facility and the moment you were diagnosed with leprosy?

10. Why did you decide to go to this health facility? (probe: who advised you to go? how did you know about it?)

Health education to community

11. What did you know about leprosy before you were diagnosed?
    - symptoms
    - cause
    - infectiousness
    - treatment
    - curability
    - social consequences

12. From where or whom did you get that knowledge?

13. What are, according to you, the most effective means to give information about leprosy to the community? Why?

14. What is your opinion on the health education on leprosy to the community as it is now given in the health facility? (probe: sufficient? satisfactory? why (not)?)

15. Do you have any suggestions for improvement concerning health education to the community?

Accessibility

16. What are/were the costs for each time you come/came to this health facility?
   - travel costs (total bus fare) ______
   - costs for accompanying persons ______
   - food and lodging ______
   - admission fee ______
   - other, specify ______

17. What is your opinion on the costs? (reasonable? too expensive?)

18. Did/do you have any problem in raising the money needed to come to the health facility? How did/do you cope?

19. How long did you have to wait (on average)? ______

Pt form nr [ ]

20. What is your opinion about the waiting time? (reasonable? too long?)

21. Do you have any suggestions for improvement concerning costs or waiting time?

Condition of facilities

22. What is your opinion about the condition of the facilities?
    - condition/cleanliness of the building
    - availability and cleanliness of toilets
    - other, specify

23. Do you have any suggestions for improvement concerning the condition of facilities?

Diagnostic procedures

When you first arrived at *this* health facility: ____________

24. How did you experience the clinical examination?
    - Was your privacy respected? (probe: how/what precautions were taken? did you need to undress? did you feel any problem?)
    - Were you examined by a person of the same sex? (F for F, M for M?) If not, was that a problem for you?

25. What is your opinion on the clinical examination? Do you have any suggestions for improvement concerning the clinical examination?

Pt form nr

Information to patients

26. What was told to you about leprosy and its treatment in the health facility?
    - about the disease 'leprosy'?
    - the duration of treatment
    - the importance of regularity of taking treatment
    - the infectiousness of leprosy (including: when infectiousness stops)
    - the curability
    - the prevention of (further) disabilities/complications
    - other, specify

27. How was the information told? (probe: per individual or in a group? enough time for giving information? was the information repeated a number of times? was the information easy to understand?)

28. What is your opinion on the information given to patients? Do you have any suggestions for improvement concerning the information given to patients?

Contact examination

29. Were your relatives invited for contact examination?
    - Did they come? (if no, why not?)
    - Did the health staff do home visits to examine your relatives?

30. What is your opinion on the examination of your relatives for leprosy (probe: important? why (not)?)

Pt form nr

Health staff

31. How was the communication between the health staff and you in this health facility? (probe: friendliness, respect for patient, sufficient time to help)

32. Do you notice any difference in the way the health staff treat leprosy patients compared to the treatment of other patients? If yes, what?

33. Are you helped by the same doctor every time? If not, is that a problem for you? Why?

34. Are you confident that the health staff that helps/helped you has sufficient knowledge of leprosy? Would they, in your opinion, need any additional training? If yes, what? Why?

35. Do you have any suggestions for improvement concerning the health staff (friendliness, continuity, training)?

Treatment

36. Is/was the medicine for leprosy always available when you come/came to get it? (probe: MDT, Prednisolon) If not always available: for how long? Where did you go instead?

Pt form nr ☐

37. Do you believe leprosy can be cured by taking the medicine? Why (not)?

38. Have you ever thought about stopping with the medicine? Why? Did you actually stop?

Ask q. 39-41 <u>only</u> to defaulting or irregular patients

39. What was the reason that you decided to stop taking the medicine?

How many times did you stop? ______

For how long did you stop? ______

Did you do anything else then? (self-treatment, traditional treatment, other doctor, etc.)

40. Did you return to treatment? Why?

If returned: did you return to the same health facility, or another? Why?

If returned to same health facility:

41. What was the reaction of the health staff? What is your opinion on the staffs' reaction?

Pt form nr ☐

Ask q. 42-43 only to patients with disabilities

42. What was done or told to you to prevent your disability/deformity from becoming worse? (probe: exercises, shoes, self-care for ulcers, care for insensitive hands and feet, sunglasses)

43. Are you afraid the disabilities will get worse? If worried: Have you discussed this with the health staff? What was their reaction? (opinion)

Stigma and socio-economic consequences

44. Did you tell anyone about your disease? (spouse, relatives, neighbours, colleagues, etc.)?

45. Does or will the disease influence your daily life? (work, partner, study) How? (did you notice any change in the behaviour of people?)

46. If worried: have you discussed this with the leprosy worker, or any other health staff? Why (not)? What did the health staff do? (opinion)

Other aspects/priorities

47. Are there any aspects of the quality of the leprosy services that are important to you, that have not already been mentioned?

Pt form nr [ ]

48. These cards represent several aspects of the quality of the leprosy services, which we have discussed. We would like to ask you to choose the three cards with the most important aspects printed on them. You can choose the aspects that deserve most priority in the leprosy services, according to your own personal opinion.

(Show and explain priority cards, tick the chosen priorities beneath)

Quality aspect	Priority?
Low costs to go to the leprosy services	
Short waiting time	
Adequate privacy during clinical examination	
Adequate information to leprosy patients on their disease	
Friendly health workers with sufficient time to help	
Adequate attention to prevention of disabilities	
Advice by leprosy workers on dealing with the social consequences of leprosy	

Would you like to ask any questions or make any comments?

____

Thank you for this interview.

Community member questionnaire **Cm form nr** ☐

Date of interview: ___

Name of interviewer: ___

Place and name of health facility: ___

'We are interviewing leprosy patients on their experiences with the different health centres in the area. However, we would also like to know the opinions of the community on these issues. We would like to ask you, as a representative of the community, some questions about the community's views on the quality of the health services offered here. These views are very important for us to know because there may be aspects of the services for leprosy patients that can still be improved. The interview will take about 45 minutes. The information you give us will be handled confidentially and your name will not be mentioned. Would you like to co-operate with this study?
If yes: 'do you mind if we take notes?'

1. Sex (M/F): ___

2. Age (in years): ___

3. Occupation: ___

Health seeking behaviour

4. If somebody has the first symptoms of leprosy (a discoloured or insensitive patch or swelling on the body), what do you think most people do to get rid of the symptoms before they go to a health facility or doctor?
(probe: self-treatment, e.g. with herbs, drugs or ointments from pharmacy, traditional care)

___

5. How long do they wait before going to a health facility or doctor? Why?

___

6. Where would they go for treatment first (private physician, dermatologist, a (sub)health centre, etc.)? Why?

___

Cm form nr [ ]

7. How much time do you think exists between the first time patients go to a doctor/health facility and the moment they are diagnosed with leprosy (on average)?

8. Why do patients go to this health facility? (probe: how do they know about it? did you know that leprosy services are offered in this health facility?)

Health education to community

9. What do people of the community in general know about leprosy?
   - symptoms
   - cause
   - infectiousness
   - treatment
   - curability
   - social consequences

10. From where or whom do they get that knowledge?

11. What are, according to you, the most effective means to give information about leprosy to the community?

Cm form nr [ ]

12. What is your opinion on the health education on leprosy to the community as it is now given in the health facility? (probe: sufficient? satisfactory?) why (not)?)

____
____
____
____

13. Do you have any suggestions for improvement concerning health education to the community?

____
____
____
____

Accessibility

14. What is your opinion on the total costs for patients, each time they come to this health facility? (travel cost, costs for accompanying persons, food and lodging, admission fee, other) Reasonable? Too expensive?

____
____
____
____

15. Do many patients have problems with raising the money needed to come to this health facility? How do they cope?

____
____
____
____

16. How long do patients have to wait (on average, as far as you know)? What is your opinion about the waiting time? (reasonable? too long?)

____
____
____
____

17. Do you have any suggestions for improvement concerning costs or waiting time?

____
____
____
____

Cm form nr [ ]

Condition of facilities

18. What is your opinion about the condition of the facilities (as far as you can say)?
    - condition/cleanliness of the building

    ______

    - availability and cleanliness of toilets

    ______

    - other, specify

    ______

19. Do you have any suggestions for improvement concerning the condition of facilities?

    ______
    ______
    ______
    ______

Diagnostic procedures

When patients arrive at the health facility for the first time:

20. What is your opinion on the clinical examination of patients (as far as you can say)?
    Is their privacy respected? (probe: how/what precautions are taken? do they feel any problems? opinion?)

    ______
    ______

    Are they examined by a person of the same sex? (F for F, M for M?)
    If not, is that a problem for them?

    ______
    ______

21. Do you have any suggestions for improvement concerning the clinical examination?

    ______
    ______
    ______
    ______

Information to patients

22. What is your/the community's opinion about the information on leprosy given to patients in the health facility (as far as you know)? (on the disease 'leprosy´, the duration of treatment, the importance of regularity of taking treatment, the infectiousness of leprosy, the curability, the prevention of disabilities, other)

23. How is the information told by the health staff? (probe: per individual or in a group?, enough time for giving information? is the information repeated a number of times? is the information easy to understand for patients?)

24. What is your opinion on the information given to patients? Do you have any suggestions for improvement concerning the information given to patients?

Contact examination

25. What is your/the community's opinion on the examination of relatives of leprosy patients for leprosy (important? why (not)?)

Health staff

26. How is the communication between the health staff and patients in this health facility? (probe: friendliness, respect for patient, sufficient time to help)

Cm form nr [ ]

27. Do you think there is any difference in the way health staff treats leprosy patients compared to the treatment of other patients? If yes, what?

28. Are you/is the community confident that the health staff that helps the patients has sufficient knowledge of leprosy? Would they, in your opinion, need any additional training? If yes, what? Why?

29. Do you have any suggestions for improvement concerning the health staff (friendliness, continuity, training)?

Treatment

30. Is the medicine for leprosy patients always available when patients come to get it? (as far as you know)

31. Do you/does the community believe leprosy can be cured by taking the medicine? Why (not)?)

Defaulting/irregular patients

32. What do you think is the reason that leprosy patients sometimes stop taking their medication?

33. Do you think they report these reasons to the health staff? Why (not)? What do you think is the reaction of the health staff? (opinion)

Stigma and socio-economic consequences

34. What social consequences does the disease have for leprosy patients in their daily lives? (work, partner, study) Is there any change in behaviour towards patients once they have been diagnosed with leprosy?

35. Do you think patients can discuss the social consequences of their disease with the leprosy workers or other health staff? Why (not)?

36. What is your opinion on the role of the health worker in this respect?

Other aspects

37. Are there any aspects of the quality of the leprosy services that are important to you, that have not already been mentioned?

Would you like to ask any questions or make any comments?

Thank you for this interview.

Health staff questionnaire **Hs form nr** [ ]

Date of interview: ______________________

Name of interviewer: ______________________

Place and name of health facility: ______________________

'We are interviewing leprosy patients on their experiences with the different health centres in the area. However, we would also like to know the opinions of the health staff on these issues. We would like to ask you some questions about the your views on the quality of the health services offered here. Your views are very important for us to know because there may be aspects of the services for leprosy patients that could still be improved. The interview will take about 45 minutes. The information you give us will be handled confidentially and your name will not be mentioned. Would you like to co-operate with this study?
If yes: 'do you mind if we take notes?'

1. Sex (M/F): ______________________

2. Age (in years): ______________________

3. Position/role in health facility: ______________________

Health seeking behaviour

4. If somebody has the first symptoms of leprosy, what do most people do to get rid of the symptoms before they go to a health facility or doctor? (probe: self-treatment, e.g. with herbs, drugs or ointments from pharmacy, traditional care)

____
____
____
____

5. How long do they wait before going to a health facility or doctor? Why?

____
____
____
____

6. Where would they go for treatment first (private physician, dermatologist, a (sub)health centre, etc.)? Why?

____
____
____
____

Hs form nr ☐

7. How much time exists between the first time patients go to a doctor/health facility and the moment they are diagnosed with leprosy (on average)?

8. Why do patients go to this health facility? (probe: how do they know about it?)

Health education to community

9. What do most patients in general know about leprosy before they are diagnosed?
   - symptoms
   - cause
   - infectiousness
   - treatment
   - curability
   - social consequences

10. From where or whom do they get that knowledge?

11. What are, according to you, the most effective means to give information about leprosy to the community?

Hs form nr

12. What action is taken to educate the community about leprosy?

13. What is your opinion on the health education on leprosy to the community as it is now given in the health facility? (probe: sufficient? satisfactory? why (not)?)

14. Do you have any suggestions for improvement concerning health education to the community?

Accessibility

15. What is your opinion on the total costs for patients, each time they come to this health facility? (travel costs, costs for accompanying persons, food and lodging, admission fee, other) Reasonable? Too expensive?

16. Do many patients have problems with raising the money needed to come to this health facility? What do/can you do?

17. How long do patients have to wait (on average)?
What is your opinion about the waiting time? (reasonable? too long?) If too long: what is the reason for long waiting times?

Hs form nr ☐

18. Do you have any suggestions for improvement concerning costs or waiting time?

Condition of facilities

19. What is your opinion about the condition of the facilities?
    - condition/cleanliness of the building
    - availability and cleanliness of toilets
    - other, specify

20. Do you have any suggestions for improvement concerning the condition of facilities?

Diagnostic procedures

When patients arrive at this health facility for the first time:

21. How do patients experience the clinical examination?
    - are precautions taken to ensure privacy? (probe: how? do patients feel any problem? opinion?)
    - Are they examined by a person of the same sex? (F for F, M for M?) If not, is that a problem for them?

22. Do you have any suggestions for improvement concerning the clinical examination?

Hs form nr ☐

Information to patients

23. What is your opinion about the information on leprosy given to patients in the health facility?
    - on the disease 'leprosy' itself
    - on the duration of treatment
    - on the importance of regularity of taking treatment
    - on the infectiousness of leprosy (including: when infectiousness stops)
    - on the curability
    - on the prevention of (further) disabilities/complications
    - other, specify

24. How is the information told? (probe: per individual or in a group?, enough time for giving information?, is the information repeated a number of times?)

25. Do patients tell you if they do not understand something about their disease or treatment?

26. What is your opinion on the information given to patients? Do you have any suggestions for improvement concerning the information given to patients?

Contact examination

27. Are relatives of patients invited for contact examination? Do they come? (if no, why not?)

Does the health staff carry out home visits to examine relatives?

28. What is your opinion on the examination of relatives of leprosy patients for leprosy (important? why (not)?)

Health staff

29. How is the communication between the health staff and patients in this health facility? (probe: opinion, sufficient time available)

30. Are patients helped by the same doctor every time? If not, is that a problem for patients?

31. In your opinion, does the health staff that helps leprosy patients have sufficient knowledge of leprosy? Would they, in your opinion, need any additional training? If yes, what? Why?

32. Do you have any suggestions for improvement concerning the health staff?

Hs form nr [ ]

Treatment

33. Is the medicine for leprosy patients always available when patients come to get it? (probe: MDT, Prednisolon) (If no, why?)

____
____
____
____

34. Do patients believe leprosy can be cured by taking the medicine? (if no, why not?)

____
____
____
____

35. What are reasons that leprosy patients sometimes stop taking their medication?

____
____
____
____

36. What do these leprosy services do to prevent patients from stopping with their medication?

____
____
____
____

Patients with disabilities

37. What is done to treat patients with disabilities?

____
____
____
____

38. Are patients in general afraid the disabilities will get worse? Do they discuss this with the health staff? What do/can you do?

____
____
____
____

Hs form nr [ ]

Stigma and socio-economic consequences

39. What social consequences does the disease have for leprosy patients in their daily lives? (work, partner, study) Is there any change in behaviour towards patients once they have been diagnosed with leprosy?

____
____
____
____

40. What is your opinion on the role of the health staff in this respect?

____
____
____
____

Other aspects

41. Are there any aspects of the quality of the leprosy services that are important to you, that have not already been mentioned?

____
____
____
____

Would you like to ask any questions or make any comments?

____
____
____
____
____
____
____
____

Thank you for this interview.

Annex 5. Priority cards

A limited number of quality aspects have been illustrated by drawings printed on cards, to make the system accessible for illiterate and low-educated respondents. On the next pages, you will find 7 priority cards. The idea is that with a marker you write the aspect represented below the drawings in the commonly used language. Make 8 copies of each page. After having made the copies, cut along the lines to separate the cards and make 8 complete sets. The 8 sets will be used during the FGDs. For the interviews with patients, only one set of cards is needed.

Priority cards

1. Low costs to go to the leprosy services
2. Short waiting time
3. Adequate privacy
4. Adequate information to leprosy patients on their disease
5. Friendly health workers with sufficient time to help
6. Adequate attention to prevention of disabilities
7. Advice by leprosy workers on dealing with the social consequences of leprosy

1. ....

2. ....

3. ....

4. ....

5.

6.

7.

Annex 6. Focus group discussions[2]

A focus group discussion (FGD) helps to explore in greater depth the findings resulting from the interviews. This enables you to obtain much valuable information on concepts, perceptions and ideas of a group, which can complement the other data. However, one should be aware that, in a group, people tend to centre their opinions on the most common ones (i.e. on 'social norms'). In reality, opinions and behaviour may be more diverse.

In this study, two FGDs with leprosy patients will be conducted in two different health facilities.

Topics
Compose a list of topics for the FGD in advance. Select 5 or 6 topics that arose during the individual interviews, which need further clarification. Both researchers should have a copy of the topics for discussion. Formulate the topics as a series of open-ended questions, for example:

Topics for FGD

1. If people find a white patch or a swelling on their body, or insensitive patches on their skin, would they seek help at a health facility/doctor straight away? If not, what could be the reason?
   Do people suspect these symptoms could be leprosy?
   Are people reluctant to go to the health centre for leprosy? If yes, why?
   Would everyone know that treatment for leprosy is free of charge?
2. What was their knowledge of leprosy before they came to the health facility? (symptoms, cause, infectiousness, treatment, curability, social consequences) Where did they get that knowledge?
   Did they ever see posters on leprosy in health centres, tv-messages, pamphlets, etc?
   Do they have any suggestions for health education to the community? What should be told?
   In their opinion, which means of giving health education are most effective? Why?
3. Etc.

[2] The information contained in this annex is based on the Health Systems Resarch modules developed by Varkevisser et al. For more detailed information, the original modules can be consulted (see key references).

Recruitment of participants

At the beginning of the study, request the co-operation of the health facilities where you would like to hold the FGDs. If they agree, ask them to invite 5 to 8 participants per FGD. This should be done timely in advance. Inform the health staff that they should explain the purpose and procedures of the FGD to the patients, and ask the patients' consent to join. Offer to refund the travel expenses if participants come specifically to join the FGD.

The discussion is facilitated when participants are roughly of the same age and socio-economic group. In some countries, it can be helpful to hold one FGD with (only) female and one with (only) male participants. The most informative discussions are those with a group of people that can express a range of views.

You could consider involving leprosy patient organisations in the FGDs. However, keep in mind that their opinions might differ from the ideas of the patient population in general. Patient organisations have access to more information and their organisations may consist mainly of older (ex)-patients, thus not representing the patient population.

Environment

Communication and interaction during the FGD should be encouraged in every way possible. Arrange chairs in a circle. Make sure there will be no disturbances, sufficient quietness, adequate lighting, etc. Try to hold the FGD in a neutral setting, which encourages participants to freely express their views. Explain to the health staff that it is preferable that they are not present during the FGDs.

Conducting the session

One researcher acts as 'facilitator' for the FGD, one is the 'recorder'. Agree in advance who will act in which of these capacities. The facilitator's role is to stimulate and support discussion. The recorder records the date, time and place, and the initials and characteristics of participants. (S)he takes notes of the opinions of participants, as much as possible in their own words, and records spontaneous relevant discussions during breaks or after the meeting has been closed. (S)he documents important aspects in the group's interaction, such as the level of participation and emotional reactions.

It is highly recommended that a tape recorder is used to assist in capturing information. However, even if a tape recorder is used, notes should also be taken, in case the machine malfunctions.

Introduce the session

The facilitator welcomes the group. Introduce yourself and introduce the recorder. Let participants introduce themselves with whatever names they wish to use. Put the participants at ease and explain the purpose of the FGD, the kind of information needed, and how the information will be used. Tell participants the information will be handled confidentially and ask them to do the same with information they will hear from the others during the session. Ask permission to use a tape recorder. You can let people hear their own voices before the session starts. Offer drinks and allow some informal discussion before the actual session starts.

Encourage discussion
Group members should discuss the topic among themselves, with guidance from the facilitator. Be enthusiastic, lively, humorous, and show your interest in the groups' ideas. Formulate questions and encourage as many participants as possible to express their views. Remember there are no 'right' or 'wrong' answers. React neutrally to both verbal and non-verbal responses. Avoid a question-and answer session. Some useful techniques to encourage involvement include:

- Asking for clarification: 'can you tell me more about…?'

- Reorienting the discussion when it goes 'off track': 'interesting point, but how about…' or use one participant's remark to direct a question to another, for example, 'Mrs. X said…, but how about you, Mrs Y?'

- When dealing with a dominant participant, try avoiding eye-contact or turning slightly away to discourage the person from speaking, or thanking the person and changing the subject

- When dealing with a reluctant participant, try using the person's name, requesting his/her opinion, making more frequent eye-contact to encourage his/her participation
- Avoid being placed in the role of expert. When asked for your ideas or views by a respondent, remember that you are not there to educate or inform. Direct the questions back to the group by saying: 'What do you think', 'What would you do?' Set aside time after the session to give participants the information they have requested

- Control the rhythm of the meeting, but in an unobtrusive way. Listen carefully, and move the discussion from topic to topic. Subtly control the time allocated to various topics so as to maintain interest. If participants spontaneously jump from one topic to another, let the discussion continue for a while, since useful additional information may surface; then summarise the points brought up and reorient the discussion

Choosing priorities
After each FGD, use the same priority card system as for the patient interviews. Give each participant his/her own set of cards. Request the participants to individually choose 3 cards with the most important quality aspects in their opinion. Ask them to explain the logic behind the chosen priorities. Write down the priorities chosen by each participant in the same way as done for the patient interviews.

Finishing the FGD
Take time at the end of the meeting to summarise the conclusions of the discussion and check for agreement. Thank the participants and let them know that their

ideas have been a valuable contribution and will be used in the end evaluations of the leprosy services.

Listen for additional comments and spontaneous discussions which occur after the meeting has been closed.

Summarising the data of the FGD

Immediately after each FGD, the facilitator and the recorder should prepare a summary which reflects the discussion as completely as possible:

1 Listen to the tape
2 Write down key statements, ideas, and attitudes expressed for each topic of discussion, using the participants' own words
3 Organise the notes according to the topic list, as sometimes participants tend to jump from topic to topic
4 Report the major findings in a narrative, following your list of topics. Include quotations whenever possible as illustrations. Include details of the selection and composition of the groups of FGD participants, and a short commentary on the group process.

Evaluate how the FGD went and what changes might be made in the topics when facilitating the next discussion.

Summary

- Select 2 health facilities for FGDs and ask health staff to invite 5-8 participants (leprosy patients)
- Compose a list of topics that need further exploration
- Find a private environment for the FGD
- Offer drinks/refreshments
- Introduce the session
- Ask permission for using tape recorder
- Recorder: take notes of discussion and group process
- Facilitator: ask the questions
- Encourage discussion
- Encourage involvement of all participants
- Move from topic to topic, taking care the discussion doesn't take too long
- Ask the participants to individually choose priorities with the cards
- Discuss priorities
- Answer questions, thank the participants
- Review the notes and listen to the tape
- Make a summary of the main findings per topic of the FGD
- Evaluate the FGD and adapt topics if necessary

Annex 7. Data analysis

Analysis of qualitative data is a matter of describing, summarising and interpreting the data. Usually, qualitative data are analysed through a thorough but time-consuming process of reviewing responses per question, coding and labelling them and listing similar responses in a category. The categorised data are then displayed in tables, for example in matrices or master sheets, after which the data are described and interpreted.

The aim of this study is, however, to gain a good *impression* of the important issues concerning client satisfaction. In the limited time available, the (limited number of) interviews have to be analysed. Therefore, a checklist for analysis has been included (annex 9), which will help in reporting the results of the study. The researchers should analyse the data by going through the checklist and answering or describing the issues raised, using the information resulting from interviews and FGDs.

In principle, the issues in the checklist can be directly discussed or described from the raw data. However, researchers who are familiar with using master sheets can compose these first, to make the data more manageable (see explanation below).

Each quality aspect will be analysed in turn. Per aspect, always try to pinpoint on which responses there is common agreement and the greatest strength of feeling. Continuously ask yourself the following questions:

- What is the most frequent response?
- Is there a trend emerging?
- What patterns surface from the data?
- What are the factors or conditions behind this common response?
- What are its causes?
- What are the effects and implications of this situation for the persons involved?
- What cause-effect relations can be derived from this situation?
- How do these relate to the broader context?
- Does the situation represent what is happening in the broader context?

The steps for data analysis are as follows:

1. Sort the data

The data of the different study populations (patients/community members/ health staff) will be analysed separately. Make three separate piles of interviews according to patients, community members and health staff.

Sort the set of patient interviews according to health facility: pile interviews held in health facility 1, pile those held in health facility 2, etc.

2. Count the scores of priority card system

Before proceeding to the actual analysis, it is useful to know the results of the priority card system first. Use both the tables resulting from the last question of the patient interviews, as well as the chosen priorities by participants of both FGDs.

Count how many times the first quality aspect (low costs to go to the leprosy services) has been ticked. Include both the results from the patients interviewed, as well as those from each participant of the FGDs. Write down the total. Do the same for the second quality aspect (short waiting time). Continue like this for each of the quality aspects.

Display the results in a table, which can be included in the report. The highest resulting sum is the most important issue, with first priority, the second highest sum represents the second priority, etc. Use these results in the description of the data.

3. Compose master sheets (optional)

Take the set of patient interviews. Per question, read the whole set of answers. Some answers from different respondents will give more or less similar information. Give the answers that belong together a label and write this in the left margin. The label should cover the content of the answers. For instance, when reviewing the answers to the question 'before you decided to go to a doctor or health facility, did you try anything at home to get rid of the symptoms?' (question 6), possible labels could be: herbs/teas, ointments, drugs pharmacy, traditional healer/herbalist, praying sessions, nothing done at home. Use not more than 6 different labels per question. Each label represents a category of answers.

Display the categories of answers in a master sheet (as headers of the columns) and include a residual category 'other: specify' for answers that do not fit into the defined categories. Include an additional category for non-response ('don't know/no answer'). In the vertical column, list the number of patients, starting with the patients interviewed at health facility 1, thereafter patients interviewed at health facility 2, etc. Tick their responses one by one in the appropriate columns.

An example of a master sheet is shown in annex 10. Under the matrix, space can be left to write details, remarks and suggested improvements.

New master sheets could also be composed for community members, and again different ones for health staff members. However, the researchers can also review the answers of community members and health staff members directly from the raw data, as there are only a few interviews.

4. Describe the data using the checklist for analysis

Describe the issues raised in the checklist belonging to the first quality aspect (health seeking behaviour). Do this systematically, taking one issue at a time. Note that the checklist is directly related to the questions in the questionnaire, and also follows the same order. Try to describe the checklist issues as accurately as possible, by revising all the respective responses given by the patients.

Some issues of the checklist are not entirely parallel to the questionnaires, but require interpretation of the responses. If it is impossible to answer a particular issue of the checklist from the collected data, then omit it. If you have made master sheets, use them for description of the data. However, take care not to make the description too 'statistical'; always include illustrations and quotations of interesting issues.

Take into account the topics discussed in the FGDs. Reread the summaries of the FGDs and reflect on whether the results of the FGD support or contrast the trends as identified in the patient interviews. Use the results of the FGDs in describing the checklist issues, but always mention which information has been derived from an FGD.

When the checklist issues relating to the first quality aspect have been answered and described for the patient group, take the set of interviews with community members. Describe their point of view on the first quality aspect, especially if striking differences occur with the responses of the patients. Then proceed to the health staff interviews. Review their answers concerning the first quality aspect, compare and contrast these with the answers of the patients and describe their views.

Having dealt with issues of the checklist belonging to the first quality aspect, and when further analysis is exhausted, move on to the next aspect (health education to community). Analyse and describe the data according to the checklist, again for the 3 study populations. In this way, move from aspect to aspect, until you have dealt with the entire checklist. Look for possible relations between data on different aspects.

'Interesting details, remarks, suggested improvements'

For the 3 groups (but especially for the patients), include interesting details and remarks, important statements, additional information or suggested improvements. Quote the respondents who elaborated on a subject, who told anecdotes, and mention the suggestions they gave. These data will often give the most interesting information and can illustrate your conclusions in the final report. Take care to include the source of the item (e.g. patient form number and health facility where (s)he was interviewed), so the information can be placed in the original context, if required.

'No answer'
Some questions may have been answered incompletely, or not at all. Other answers may be clearly inconsistent or vague. If data are of doubtful quality, exclude this particular part of the data from further analysis. Discuss the parts you have excluded in your report.

5. Report results
Reread the objectives of the study: this is what has to become clear in the report. Data analysis and the writing of the report take place simultaneously. Summarise or edit the description of the data to short narratives about each quality aspect, for each study population separately (see example below).

Compare and contrast the experiences of patients with those of community members and health staff (on which issues do the groups agree? on what topics do they have different opinions?). Include the results of the priority card system (how important is a particular quality aspect for patients?).

Always mention the amount of respondents who gave similar responses. Include quotations of remarks and details to illustrate conclusions. Sometimes individual respondents can give interesting comments ('eye-openers'). Describe or quote these comments, but always mention the amount of patients who gave that information.

In principle, analyse the health facilities jointly. However, mention important differences that occur between health facilities. Try not to 'accuse' health facilities if patients have complaints. Be neutral, acknowledge that a problem exists that needs improvement.

When you have finished reporting the results on a particular quality aspect, give a short summary (2-3 sentences) of the main conclusions discussed. List the suggested improvements, including the amount and type of respondent that gave the suggestion (patients/community members/health staff /participants of FGDs) and, if relevant, the various health facilities.

Example

Accessibility - costs
Travel costs seem to cause problems for patients, especially for those who have to travel from their home to the referral hospital. Bus tickets mostly cost 1 R$ one way, making the total costs of a visit about 2 to 3 R$ (13pts). This amount is a problem for some patients. Four patients said that they cope by borrowing money, one tries to come by bike (he is disabled!). Another patient used to be accompanied by his wife, but he had to leave her behind, and still he sometimes just cannot come because it is too expensive. Especially for patients who are on health leave or don't have a job (mostly because of the disease), it is very difficult to come. Three patients said that they are expected several times at the health centre for visits to the doctor, the psychologist, the physiotherapist or for lab results. Five of the 19 patients receive or try to get bus tickets from the health centre, which helps a lot (health facility 1,2,4). A patient

who participated in an FGD remarked that she was trying to get this bus pass, but that she doesn't know if she will succeed as she has to come so often (every 2 weeks to the physiotherapist and every month for treatment).

Patients coming by car (3 pts) spend more money (for fuel), but it seems that these patients have less problems in acquiring this money. The fact that they have a car might signify that they have more economical resources. One patient remarked that each time he comes for treatment he loses a working day and thus the income, meaning that it costs him 60 to 70 R$ per visit.

When asked to choose priorities, low costs were ranked fourth in the list of priorities. It is considered important, but if compared to the other factors (such as information to the patients, friendly health workers), patients seem to give those aspects a higher priority than low costs.

Community members remark that the facilities are easily accessible by public transport. However, one community member mentioned that her relative is very old and cannot travel by bus. A taxi is too expensive and neighbours wouldn't bring him because he has leprosy. Therefore, an ambulance has to be asked to pick him up and bring him to the health centre. Two community members interviewed agreed that for old or handicapped people, transport is a problem. They have to pay for the bus, whereas most patients can just walk to the health centre. Not having a job is also mentioned as a factor causing lack of ability to afford bus tickets, even if the price is reasonable. A member of the patient organisation said in that case they can go to the municipality where the social worker can pay the travel costs.

Health staff members also share the opinion that their health facilities are easily accessible (and therefore in some cases are chosen as referral centres for the leprosy programme). However, the costs are a problem because lots of patients are very poor; the travel costs are high in comparison to what they earn. According to them, these patients are given bus tickets (in health facility 1, 2 and 4). In health facility 6, bus tickets are provided through the municipality. Health staff members consider this as an important factor, as patients sometimes come 1 or 2 weeks late for their medicine because they have first to obtain money. So providing bus tickets is a way of preventing patients from defaulting.

Conclusion
Travel costs can be considered an obstacle for patients visiting the health facility (especially the referral hospital). Providing bus tickets helps the poorer patients a lot, especially those who are old and disabled.

Suggested improvements:
- The municipality should give bus tickets for patients (2 pts, 2 part FGD, 2 cm, HF 1,2,3,5)
- Treatment should be available closer to peoples houses (3 pts, HF 2,4, 1 hs HF 3)

Summary

- Make separate piles of patient interviews, community member interviews and health staff interviews
- Sort the patient interviews according to health facility
- From the set of patient interviews and FGDs, compose a list of priorities in order of importance following the priority card system
- Optional: compose master sheets for the patient interviews, and if needed, for the community member and health staff interviews
- Use the checklist for analysis to interpret and analyse the data of the patient interviews (and FGDs, if the subject has been discussed) on the first quality aspect
- Use the checklist for analysing the community member interviews on the first quality aspect
- Use the checklist for analysing the health staff member interviews on the first quality aspect
- Move to the next quality aspects and use the checklist for describing the data for each study population
- When all quality aspects have been completed, summarise or edit main results in narratives per study population, always including the amount of respondents who gave similar answers, as well as the health facilities, where relevant
- After describing the results of each quality aspect, list the main conclusions in a few sentences and list the suggested improvements by the respondents (including amount and type of respondents who gave similar suggestions, as well as the health facilities, where relevant)

Annex 8. Example of a master sheet

Patient interviews, health seeking behaviour
Question 6

Patient Nr.	Herbs teas	Ointments	Drugs pharmacy	Traditional healer/ herbalist	Praying session	Nothing done at home	Other: specify Don't know/ no answer
1 (HF1)							
2 (HF1)							
3 (HF1)							
4 (HF1)							
5 (HF2)							
6 (HF2)							
7 (HF2)							
8 (HF3)							
9 (HF3)							
10 (HF3)							
11 (HF3)							
12 (HF4)							
13 (HF4)							
14 (HF4)							
15 (HF4)							
16 (HF5)							
17 (HF5)							
18 (HF5)							
19 (HF5)							
20 (HF6)							
21 (HF6)							
22 (HF6)							
Total							

Details/remarks:

Suggested improvements:

Annex 9. Checklist for analysis

The issues in italics are general issues. These should be discussed in the report by answering the more specific questions beneath them.

Background variables

What are the characteristics of your respondents? Is the sample representative for the study population?

Patient interviews (questions 1-5, 38):

- How many male patients did you interview? How many females?
- How many patients were between 15 and 45? How many were older than 45 years?
- How many patients had PB leprosy, how many MB?
- How many patients had just started treatment (taken less than 3 doses), how many had longer experience with the health services? How many were RFT?
- How many patients with disabilities did you interview?
- How many defaulting or irregular patients did you interview? (question 38)
- Is the sample of leprosy patients interviewed representative for the patient population?

FGDs:

- How many male patients participated in each FGD? How many females?
- How many patients had PB leprosy, how many MB?
- How many participants had disabilities?
- How many had defaulted or were irregular?
- Is the selection of participants representative for the patient population?

Community members (questions 1-3):

- What was the sex, age and occupation of the community members interviewed in each health facility?

Health staff (questions 1-3):

- What was the sex, age and position of the health staff members interviewed in each health facility?

Health seeking behaviour

What do people tend to do first when they discover the first symptoms of leprosy? Why?

Patient interviews (question 6) and FGDs (if discussed):

- Which action (use of herbs, ointments, teas, drugs from pharmacy, visit to traditional healers, praying sessions, etc) was most frequently mentioned by the patients?
- How many patients mentioned this action?
- Which other actions were mentioned? By how many patients?
- How many patients went directly to a health facility or doctor (including private physicians)?

Community members (question 4):

- Did the community members mention striking differences on this subject, if compared to the patients? What?

Health staff (question 4):

- Did the health staff members mention striking differences on this subject, if compared to the patients? What?

What is the average time patients wait before deciding to go to a health facility or doctor (patient delay)? Why do they wait? Why do they finally go? Where do they go?

Patient interviews (questions 7,8) and FGDs (if discussed):

- How many patients waited less than 3 months before going to a health facility or doctor?
- How many waited longer than 1 year? How long?
- Why do these patients wait with seeking (bio)medical help?
- Can you identify differences between patients who go directly to a health facility/doctor and patients who wait (e.g. literacy/illiteracy, males/females, serious/less serious symptoms, poor/less poor patients, etc.)
- Why do patients who delay finally decide to go to a health facility/doctor?
- Where do they tend to go first (private doctor, health centre, hospital, etc.)?

Community members (question 6):

- Did the community members mention striking differences on this subject, if compared to the patients? What?

Health staff (question 6):

- Did the health staff members mention striking differences on this subject, if compared to the patients? What?

Are patients diagnosed with leprosy immediately or do doctors/health workers/ private physicians/etc. sometimes misdiagnose the symptoms (doctors delay)?

Patient interviews (question 8, 9) and FGDs (if discussed):

- How many patients were diagnosed less than 3 months after going to a health facility or doctor for the first time with this disease?
- How many were diagnosed 1 year or longer after going to a health facility or doctor for the first time with this disease? How long?

- Can you identify a difference in adequacy of diagnosing leprosy between private doctors and public health services?
- How many patients were misdiagnosed once? How many twice or more? With what other diseases were they diagnosed?

Community members (question 7):
- Did the community members mention striking differences on this subject, if compared to the patients? What?

Health staff (question 7):
- Did the health staff members mention striking differences on this subject, if compared to the patients? What?
- Did they mention misdiagnoses by doctors/health workers as a problem?
- What is the reason they gave for misdiagnoses?

Why do patients decide to go to the health facility where they are currently treated? What is the reputation of the health facility?

Patient interviews (question 10) and FGDs (if discussed):
- Why did the patients decide to go to the health facility where they are currently treated? (how many were referred by other doctors, how many already knew the health facility, how many had heard about it from relatives/other leprosy patients, etc.)
- Are there significant differences between the health facilities visited during the study as regards how they are known in the community?

Community members (question 8):
- Did the community members mention striking differences on this subject, if compared to the patients? What?

Health staff (question 8):
- Did the health staff members mention striking differences on this subject, if compared to the patients? What?

All:
- Were other interesting remarks or details given on this subject? What?
- Were any suggestions for improvement given on this topic? What? By whom? (pt/part FGD/cm/hs?)

Health education to community

What do patients (before diagnosis)/the community know about leprosy? With what do they associate leprosy?

Patient interviews (question 11) and FGDs (if discussed):
- Were there any patients who had never heard of leprosy?
- With what symptoms do patients relate ‘leprosy’?
- What is thought to be the cause of ‘leprosy’?

- Did they know that leprosy can be transmitted? How many did? How did they think it is transmitted?
- Did they know leprosy can be treated, and how?
- Did they know leprosy is curable? How many did?
- What did they know about the stigma and social consequences of leprosy?

Community members (question 9):
- Did the community members mention striking differences on this subject, if compared to the patients? What?

Health staff (question 9):
- Did the health staff members mention striking differences on this subject, if compared to the patients? What?

From where do people get that knowledge?

Patient interviews (question 12) and FGDs (if discussed):
- What were the most frequent ways of acquiring knowledge of leprosy (even if the information is not medically correct)? (heard in community, from other patients, tv, radio, posters, lectures, etc.)
- How many patients mentioned this way of having heard about leprosy?
- Which other ways were mentioned? By how many patients?

Community members (question 10):
- Did the community members mention striking differences on this subject, if compared to the patients? What?

Health staff (question 10):
- Did the health staff members mention striking differences on this subject, if compared to the patients? What?

What are effective methods for health education according to the different study populations? Why those methods? (discuss per method mentioned)

Patient interviews (question 13) and FGDs (if discussed):
- What method was mentioned most often? (tv, radio, posters, pamphlets, street theatre, lectures, school health programs, etc.) By how many patients? Why did they choose this method?
- What other methods were mentioned? Why those methods? By how many patients?

Community members (question 11):
- Did the community members mention striking differences on this subject, if compared to the patients? What?

Health staff (question 11):
- Did the health staff members mention striking differences on this subject, if compared to the patients? What?

What is the general opinion/satisfaction as regards the health education provided by the services? Does the available health education contribute to the awareness of people on leprosy?

How does the health seeking behaviour of patients relate to the health education given on leprosy to the community? (do they go to the health facilities directly when they have symptoms?)

Patient interviews (question 14) and FGDs (if discussed):
- Did the provided health education contribute to their knowledge of leprosy before they were diagnosed? (relate to questions 6,7)
- Did patients who had seen or heard health education about leprosy before they were diagnosed, suspect they had leprosy themselves? (relate to questions 6,7)
- Did they go to the health facility directly? Why or why not? (relate to questions 6,7)
- What is the patients' opinion on the health education to the community as is presently given by the health facility? Is it, according to them, satisfactory?

Community members (question 12):
- Did the community members mention striking differences on this subject, if compared to the patients? What?

Health staff (question 13):
- Which action is taken to give health education to the community?
- Did the health staff members mention striking differences on this subject, if compared to the patients? What?

All:
- Were other interesting remarks or details given on this subject? What?
- Were any suggestions for improvement given on this topic? What? By whom? (pt/part FGD/cm/hs?)

Accessibility - costs
Are the costs patients have to pay for going to the health facility a problem/ obstacle? Why?

Patient interviews (questions 16,17,18) and FGDs (if discussed):
- What is the range of costs patients have to make for going to the health facility? What type of costs cause most problems (travel costs, costs for accompanying persons, lodging and feeding, admission fee, treatment costs, etc.)? For how many patients?
- Are there significant differences in costs between the health facilities?
- What is the patients' opinion on the costs to go to the health facility? Are the costs reasonable?
- Can they cope with raising the money? How?
- Are the costs a reason for them not to come to the health facility sometimes? Does this differ per health facility?
- What is the importance of low costs for patients? (see results priority cards)

Community members (question 14,15):
- Did the community members mention striking differences on this subject, if compared to the patients? What?

Health staff (question 15,16):
- Did the health staff members mention striking differences on this subject, if compared to the patients? What?
- Does/can the health staff do anything to help poor patients in this respect?

All:
- Were other interesting remarks or details given on this subject? What?
- Were any suggestions for improvement given on this topic? What? By whom? (pt/part FGD/cm/hs?)

Accessibility - waiting time
Do patients have to wait a long time before they are helped?

Patient interviews (question 19,20) and FGDs (if discussed):
- How many patients waited less than 20 minutes (on average), how many patients waited more than 1 hour? How long? Does this differ per health facility?
- What is their opinion on the waiting times?
- Are long waiting times a problem for patients? Why?
- How important is a short waiting time to the patients? (see results priority cards)

Community members (question 16):
- Did the community members mention striking differences on this subject, if compared to the patients? What?

Health staff (question 17):
- Did the health staff members mention striking differences on this subject, if compared to the patients? What?
- With what do they relate long waiting times?

All:
- Were other interesting remarks or details given on this subject? What?
- Were any suggestions for improvement given on this topic? What? By whom? (pt/part FGD/cm/hs?)

Condition of facilities
How is the condition of the health facilities? Are the facilities satisfactory?

Patient interviews (question 22) and FGDs (if discussed):
- Did patients mention the condition or cleanliness of the facilities is as being insufficient? How many patients? In what respect?
- Were there significant differences between the health facilities?

Community members (question 18):
- Did the community members mention striking differences on this subject, if compared to the patients? What?

Health staff (question 19):
- Did the health staff members mention striking differences on this subject, if compared to the patients? What?

All:
- Were other interesting remarks or details given on this subject? What?
- Were any suggestions for improvement given on this topic? What? By whom? (pt/part FGD/cm/hs?)

Diagnostic procedures
Is the patient's privacy respected?

Patient interviews (question 24,25) and FGDs (if discussed):
- What precautions are taken to ensure privacy (especially when patients have to undress)?
- Do patients feel their privacy is respected? How many encountered problems with respect for their privacy? Why?
- Is a health worker of the opposite sex viewed as a problem by the patient? By how many? What is being done to solve this?
- Is there a significant difference between the health facilities?
- Is privacy a priority issue according to patients? (see results priority cards)

Community members (question 20):
- Did the community members mention striking differences on this subject, if compared to the patients? What?

Health staff (question 21):
- Did the health staff members mention striking differences on this subject, if compared to the patients? What?

All:
- Were other interesting remarks or details given on this subject? What?
- Were any suggestions for improvement given on this topic? What? By whom? (pt/part FGD/cm/hs?)

Information to patients
Is adequate information given to patients on leprosy, in such a way that they can understand?

Patient interviews (question 26, 27, 28) and FGDs (if discussed):
- What is told to patients/what do they remember from what is told about the disease 'leprosy'?
- What is told to patients/what do they remember from what is told about the duration of treatment and the importance of taking medicine regularly?

- What is told to patients/what do they remember from what is told about infectiousness and when it stops?
- What is told to patients/what do they remember from what is told about curability?
- What is told to patients/what do they remember from what is told about POD?
- How many patients were given information in a group-setting? How many were informed individually?
- Does the doctor/health worker give adequate information, in a patient manner and in accordance with the patients' educational level?
- Is the information generally repeated?
- Is the information easy to understand for patients?
- Is sufficient time taken to give proper explanation?
- Do significant differences exist between the information given in the different health facilities?
- Are patients satisfied with the information given?
- How important do the patients view this information? (see results priority cards)

Community members (question 22,23,24):
- Did the community members mention striking differences on this subject, if compared to the patients? What?

Health staff (question 23,24,25,26):
- Did the health staff members mention striking differences on this subject, if compared to the patients? What?

All:
- Were other interesting remarks or details given on this subject? What?
- Were any suggestions for improvement given on this topic? What? By whom? (pt/part FGD/cm/hs?)

Contact examination

Are relatives systematically invited for contact examination? How is contact examination experienced?

Patient interviews (question 29,30) and FGDs (if discussed):
- How many patients were informed about the necessity of contact examination? Was there any difference between the health facilities in the tracing of contacts?
- How many patients had relatives that actually came for examination? Why, or why not?
- How many patients had relatives that were visited and examined by health staff?
- What is the patients' opinion on contact examination? Are they afraid they could transmit the disease to their relatives? How many think it is important, how many think it is not? Why?

Community members (question 25):
- Did the community members mention striking differences on this subject, if compared to the patients? What?

Health staff (question 27,28):
- Did the health staff members mention striking differences on this subject, if compared to the patients? What?

All:
- Were other interesting remarks or details given on this subject? What?
- Were any suggestions for improvement given on this topic? What? By whom? (pt/part FGD/cm/hs?)

Health staff - attitude
How is the attitude of health staff towards the patients?

Patient interviews (question 31,32) and FGDs (if discussed):
- How many patients were of the opinion that the communication between them and the health staff was good? Why?
- How many patients had any complaints about the attitude of the health staff? What?
- Are leprosy patients treated equally to other patients?
- Do patients think sufficient time was taken/available for them? How many did, how many didn't?
- Can you identify significant differences between the health facilities with respect to the attitude of the staff?
- How important are friendly and patient health workers for the patients? (see results priority cards)

Community members (question 26,27):
- Did the community members mention striking differences on this subject, if compared to the patients? What?

Health staff (question 29):
- Did the health staff members mention striking differences on this subject, if compared to the patients? What?

All:
- Were other interesting remarks or details given on this subject? What?
- Were any suggestions for improvement given on this topic? What? By whom? (pt/part FGD/cm/hs?)

Health staff - continuity
Is the medical care continuous?

Patient interviews (question 33) and FGDs (if discussed):
- How many patients were helped by the same health staff member every time?
- How many were helped by different health staff members? Did they experience this as a problem? Why, or why not?
- Do health staff members handover the history of patients adequately?

Health staff (question 30):
- Did the health staff members mention striking differences on this subject, if compared to the patients? What?

All:
- Were other interesting remarks or details given on this subject? What?
- Were any suggestions for improvement given on this topic? What? By whom? (pt/part FGD/cm/hs?)

Health staff – technical competence
Are health professionals properly trained in leprosy? Do patients feel confident about their technical competence?

Patient interviews (question 34) and FGDs (if discussed):
- How many patients felt confident that the health staff helping them has sufficient knowledge of leprosy?
- How many patients had doubts? Why?
- Is there a relation between experienced misdiagnoses and patient doubts as to their health providers' technical competence? (relate to question 8)

Community members (question 28):
- Did the community members mention striking differences on this subject, if compared to the patients? What?

Health staff (question 31):
- Did the health staff members mention striking differences on this subject, if compared to the patients? What?
- Do they receive sufficient training on leprosy?

All:
- Were other interesting remarks or details given on this subject? What?
- Were any suggestions for improvement given on this topic? What? By whom? (pt/part FGD/cm/hs?)

Treatment
Do health services always have sufficient medication stocks?

Patient interviews (question 36) and FGDs (if discussed):
- How many patients found MDT to be unavailable when they came for treatment?
- How many patients found Prednisolon to be unavailable when they came to get it?
- For how long was the medicine out of stock?
- Where did they get the medicine instead?
- Were there significant differences between the health facilities with respect to the availability of medicine?
- Was lack of medicine a reason for patients to stop taking the medicine for some time? How many had to stop for this reason?

Community members (question 30):
- Did the community members mention striking differences on this subject, if compared to the patients? What?

Health staff (question 33):
- Did the health staff members mention striking differences on this subject, if compared to the patients? What?
- For what reason is the medicine sometimes out of stock?

Do patients believe the medicine really cures leprosy?

Patient interviews (question 37) and FGDs (if discussed):
- How many patients believe they will be cured when taking the medicine?
- How many have doubts? Why?
- Can a relation be identified between not believing the medicine will cure them and the quality of information given to the patients? (relate to question 26, 27)
- Does a relation exist between not believing the medicine will cure them and defaulting/irregularity? (relate to question 38)

Community members (question 31):
- Did the community members mention striking differences on this subject, if compared to the patients? What?

Health staff (question 34):
- Did the health staff members mention striking differences on this subject, if compared to the patients? What?

All:
- Were other interesting remarks or details given on this subject? What?
- Were any suggestions for improvement given on this topic? What? By whom? (pt/part FGD/cm/hs?)

Defaulting/irregular patients
Why do patients think about stopping with the medicine?
What are reasons for patients defaulting or coming irregularly for treatment?
Which of these reasons have to do with the quality of the health services? How is the issue of defaulting or irregular patients dealt with, and how is that perceived?

Patient interviews (question 39,40,41) and FGDs (if discussed):
- How many patients ever thought about stopping with their medicine? Why?
- How many of them did not really stop taking the medicine? Why?
- How many of them defaulted or became irregular? What are the reasons to default treatment (feeling cured, think medicine does not help, work, travel, side-effects, etc.)?
- Does their defaulting or not coming regularly for treatment relate to improper information given to patients? (relate to question 26,27)
- How many of the defaulting/irregular patients returned to treatment? Why?

- Does this relate to some action of the health services (letter, phone call, home visit)?
- How many patients were invited back to treatment by the health facility? How?
- Did they return to treatment at the same health facility? If not, why not?
- What is the reaction of the staff when a patient has defaulted or does not come regularly for treatment? Do these patients get extra attention and information? What other actions are taken? What are the patients' opinions on these actions?

Community members (question 32,33):
- Did the community members mention striking differences on this subject, if compared to the patients? What?

Health staff (question 35,36):
- Did the health staff members mention striking differences on this subject, if compared to the patients? What?

All:
- Were other interesting remarks or details given on this subject? What?
- Were any suggestions for improvement given on this topic? What? By whom? (pt/part FGD/cm/hs?)

Prevention of disabilities

What is done to prevent disabilities from becoming worse? How are the social/ psychological consequences of disabled patients dealt with, and how is that perceived?

Patient interviews (question 42,43) and FGDs (if discussed):
- How many patients received adequate treatment and information/education on their disability (depending on the disability: exercises, shoes, self-care for ulcers, care for insensitive hands/feet, sunglasses)?
- For how many was this aspect of treatment unsatisfactory?
- Is there a difference between the health facilities?
- How many patients were worried about their disability?
- How many of them reported this to the health staff?
- What did the health staff do? Was the reaction perceived as positive? Did this help the patient?
- How important is POD for patients? (see results priority cards)

Health staff (question 37,38):
- Did the health staff members mention striking differences on this subject, if compared to the patients? What?

All:
- Were other interesting remarks or details given on this subject? What?
- Were any suggestions for improvement given on this topic? What? By whom? (pt/part FGD/cm/hs?)

Stigma and socio-economic consequences

Do patients tell others about their disease? Is stigma against leprosy a problem? How does this reveal itself in the daily lives of patients? Does the disease have social or economical consequences? How does the health staff deal with these problems and how is that perceived?

Patient interviews (question 44,45,46) and FGDs (if discussed):

- How many patients told others about their disease?
- What kind of social consequences does the disease have for patients (work, study, partner, etc.)? How many patients experience such consequences?
- What psychological impact does the disease have on the lives of patients (including self-stigmatisation)?
- If patients' lives are affected by their disease, do they report this to the health staff? How many?
- What was the reaction of the staff when a patient tells them about their problems?
- Did they get extra attention and information? What other actions were taken? What were the patients' opinions on these reactions?
- How important is advice on dealing with the social consequences of leprosy for patients? (see results priority cards)

Community members (question 34,35,36):

- Did the community members mention striking differences on this subject, if compared to the patients? What?

Health staff (question 39,40):

- Did the health staff members mention striking differences on this subject, if compared to the patients? What?

All:

- Were other interesting remarks or details given on this subject? What?
- Were any suggestions for improvement given on this topic? What? By whom? (pt/part FGD/cm/hs?)

Other aspects/priorities

List additional aspects of the quality of leprosy services, and add by which type of respondent it was mentioned (pts: question 47, cm: question 37, hs: question 41).

Patient interviews, question 48:

Count how many times each quality aspect has been ticked. Include both the results from the patients interviewed, as well as those from each participant of the FGDs. Display results in a table as explained in annex 7.

Annex 10. Format for a 'client satisfaction' report

Section	Topics	Pages
Front page		1
Contents		1/2
Executive summary	• Short description methodology • Main findings and conclusions • 5-7 most significant recommendations	1
List of abbreviations		1
Introduction	• Aim of the study • Period in which the study took place • Members of research team	1/2
Methodology	• Districts and health facilities visited • Sampling procedures • Number of interviews and FGDs • Description of study population • Practical and methodological problems • Short evaluation of experiences with the study	1 1/2
Results	• Overview of the results per quality aspect: - Health seeking behaviour - Health education to community - Accessibility (costs, waiting time) - Condition of facilities - Diagnostic procedures - Information to patients - Contact examination - Health staff (attitude, continuity, technical competence) - Treatment (including dealing with non-compliance) - POD - Stigma and socio-economic consequences	8
Conclusions and recommendations		2
Annexes	• References • Schedule of the study activities • Map of health facilities visited • Results of priority card system • FGD topics used • Summary of discussion with programme staff • Questionnaires (optional)	